Dear Parents and Educators,

Welcome to Penguin Young Readers! As parents and educators, you know that each child develops at his or her own pace—in terms of speech, critical thinking, and, of course, reading. Penguin Young Readers recognizes this fact. As a result, each Penguin Young Readers book is assigned a traditional easy-to-read level (1–4) as well as a Guided Reading Level (A–P). Both of these systems will help you choose the right book for your child. Please refer to the back of each book for specific leveling information. Penguin Young Readers features esteemed authors and illustrators, stories about favorite characters, fascinating nonfiction, and more!

Titanic: The Story Lives On!

LEVEL **4**

GUIDED READING LEVEL **N**

This book is perfect for a **Fluent Reader** who:
- can read the text quickly with minimal effort;
- has good comprehension skills;
- can self-correct (can recognize when something doesn't sound right); and
- can read aloud smoothly and with expression.

Here are some **activities** you can do during and after reading this book:
- Comprehension: Answer the following questions about the story:
  - Where did the *Titanic* leave from? Where was it headed?
  - What caused the *Titanic* to sink?
  - How could this disaster have been avoided?
  - Why did Dr. Ballard want to keep the location of the wreck a secret?
- Creative Writing: Imagine that you were a passenger on the *Titanic*. Write a story describing your experience on the ship. Be sure to include details: Were you rich or poor? Where were you when the disaster struck? How did you feel? How were you rescued?

Remember, sharing the love of reading with a child is the best gift you can give!

—Bonnie Bader, EdM
  Penguin Young Readers program

*Penguin Young Readers are leveled by independent reviewers applying the standards developed by Irene Fountas and Gay Su Pinnell in *Matching Books to Readers: Using Leveled Books in Guided Reading*, Heinemann, 1999.

For Bridget O'Driscoll of Ballydehob,
County Cork, Ireland, third-class passenger
aboard *Titanic*. She was rescued in
Collapsible Lifeboat D—LD

Penguin Young Readers
Published by the Penguin Group
Penguin Group (USA) Inc., 375 Hudson Street, New York, New York 10014, USA
Penguin Group (Canada), 90 Eglinton Avenue East, Suite 700, Toronto, Ontario M4P 2Y3, Canada
(a division of Pearson Penguin Canada Inc.)
Penguin Books Ltd., 80 Strand, London WC2R 0RL, England
Penguin Group Ireland, 25 St. Stephen's Green, Dublin 2, Ireland (a division of Penguin Books Ltd.)
Penguin Group (Australia), 250 Camberwell Road, Camberwell, Victoria 3124, Australia
(a division of Pearson Australia Group Pty. Ltd.)
Penguin Books India Pvt. Ltd., 11 Community Centre, Panchsheel Park, New Delhi—110 017, India
Penguin Group (NZ), 67 Apollo Drive, Rosedale, Auckland 0632, New Zealand
(a division of Pearson New Zealand Ltd.)
Penguin Books (South Africa) (Pty.) Ltd., 24 Sturdee Avenue,
Rosebank, Johannesburg 2196, South Africa

Penguin Books Ltd., Registered Offices: 80 Strand, London WC2R 0RL, England

Text copyright © 2012 by Laura Driscoll. Illustrations © 2012 by Bob Kayganich. Published by Penguin
Young Readers, an imprint of Penguin Group (USA) Inc., 345 Hudson Street, New York, New York 10014.
Manufactured in China.

Library of Congress Control Number: 2011018013

ISBN 978-0-448-45757-4 (pbk)   10 9 8 7 6 5 4 3 2 1
ISBN 978-0-448-45902-8 (HC)   10 9 8 7 6 5 4 3 2 1

PENGUIN YOUNG READERS

LEVEL
FLUENT
READER
4

TITANIC
The Story Lives On!

by Laura Driscoll
illustrated by Bob Kayganich
and with photographs

Penguin Young Readers
An Imprint of Penguin Group (USA) Inc.

Chapter 1

September 1, 1985, 12:00 AM

It is the middle of the night in the middle of the Atlantic Ocean. Aboard a ship, several crew members are awake. Throughout the night, they search for sunken treasure.

What exactly are they looking for?

Is it a chest of gold and jewels? No!

They are hoping to find the *RMS Titanic*. The famous ship has been lost since 1912.

The *Titanic* was huge—longer than two football fields and as tall as an 11-story building.

So why is it so hard to find? No one knows exactly where the *Titanic* sank. In 1912, its crew sent out messages with its position. But was it correct? Also, the ship sank so long ago. The wreck may have rusted away to nothing by now.

If the wreck remains, it lies on the ocean floor about two and a half miles down. There has been no good way to search for it at such depths . . . until now.

Scientists study video screens for signs of the *Titanic*.

The ship is towing a deep-sea sub called *Argo*. No people are inside *Argo*, but it has video cameras. Scientists on the ship can watch what *Argo* films on video screens. They have been watching around the clock for about a week. So far, all they've seen is a lot of mud.

Suddenly, just after 1:00 AM, a crew member points at a video screen. "There's something!" he says.

The ship's huge boilers burned coal to power the engines.

At first they see pieces of metal. Then they see a huge boiler from a steamship. Before long they see the bow (front) of the ship itself!

They've found the *Titanic*! The team claps, cheers, and celebrates!

The bow of the *Titanic* is covered in rust after 73 years underwater.

But they also take a silent moment to remember the tragedy. It was at about this time that the *Titanic* sank. At 2:20 AM on April 15, 1912, around 1,500 people lost their lives.

Chapter 2

In 1912, the only way to cross the Atlantic was by ship. The trip took nearly six days. Shipping companies tried to outdo one another. Each new ocean liner was the fastest, the biggest, or the best in some way.

The *Titanic* was named after the Titans, giants from Greek myths. Brand-new in 1912, it was the largest ship ever built. Just one of its propellers was four times taller than a man and heavier than five elephants. (The wing propellers were 23 feet across and weighed about 38 tons each.)

A giant propeller on the *Titanic*

The *Titanic* wasn't just the biggest. It had the best of everything. It had fancy restaurants and cafés, two libraries, a gym, and a swimming pool. One suite cost $4,500 for a one-way ticket. Back then a person could buy four houses with that much money!

The pool was one of the first ever on an ocean liner.

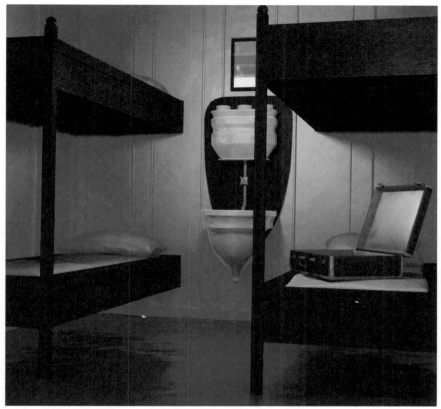

A third-class cabin on the *Titanic*

Not all the passengers were rich. Some were very poor. They were coming to the United States to find a better life. These passengers paid $36.25 for a bed in a third-class cabin.

The *Titanic* pulls away from the dock.

At noon on April 10, 1912, the ship left Southampton, England, on its first voyage ever. As the *Titanic* steamed out to sea, a large crowd cheered and waved from the shore. It was due to arrive in New York City on April 17.

No one expected an accident at sea. The *Titanic*'s builders said it was "designed to be unsinkable." The *Titanic* had watertight compartments on the lowest level. These compartments helped to keep ships afloat. The *Titanic* had 16. As many as four compartments could flood and be sealed off. The *Titanic* would still float.

crow's nest

stern

bow

watertight compartments

After three days at sea, the ship was making good time. Then, on April 14, radio messages from other ships warned of icebergs in the area. These huge mountains of ice could be a deadly

threat to ships. Even so, the *Titanic* steamed ahead, nearly at top speed.

Frederick Fleet was on watch that night. It was freezing cold. The sea was calm. The moon wasn't out.

At 11:40 PM, Fleet suddenly made out something looming ahead. He rang the alarm bell three times.

"Iceberg right ahead!" he called.

The crew tried to turn the ship and avoid the iceberg. But it was too late. Under the water, the jagged iceberg ripped open the starboard (right) side of the *Titanic*. Right away, six of the watertight compartments began flooding. That was too many for the *Titanic* to remain afloat.

The "unsinkable" *Titanic* was sinking! More than 2,200 people were onboard. The ship was about 400 miles from land.

Even worse, there were not enough lifeboats. The ship had 20 lifeboats. But it would have needed almost twice as many to save everyone.

The crew hurried to help passengers into lifeboats. At first, passengers did not want to leave the *Titanic*. It did not appear damaged—yet. People were scared to get into small lifeboats and be lowered into the icy sea.

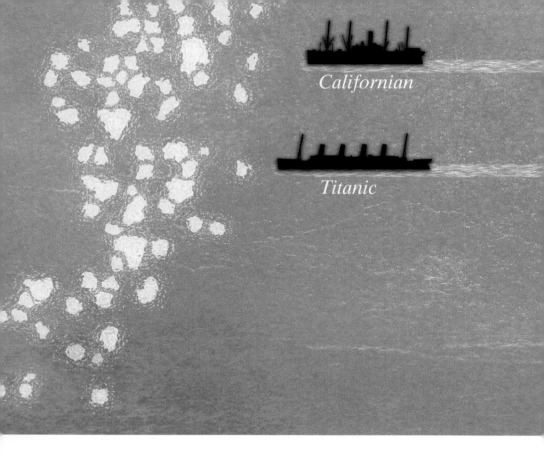

Californian

Titanic

Meanwhile, SOS messages were sent to other ships. An SOS is a code that means "Help! Emergency!"

The *Californian* was only 15 miles away. It could have reached the *Titanic* before it sank. But the radio operator had gone to bed. The radio was off.

Carpathia

The *Californian* never heard the *Titanic*'s calls for help.

The *RMS Carpathia* heard the call at 12:35 AM. Right away, it headed toward the sinking ship. But the *Carpathia* was 58 miles away. Its top speed was just 20 miles per hour.

The *Titanic* had been slowly sinking for three hours. By 2:18 AM, the stern (back) rose up so that the ship was almost on end. Within two minutes, it slid into the icy water.

The *Titanic* was gone.

The *Carpathia* arrived at 4:00 AM. The 706 passengers in lifeboats were rescued. But about 1,500 people were lost at sea.

Both photos show the *Titanic* survivors safely onboard the *Carpathia*.

The sinking was front-page news around the world. It was a giant disaster made from many small things that went wrong. What if there had been a bright moon that night? Perhaps the lookout would have seen the iceberg in time for the ship to change course. What if there had been more lifeboats? What if the *Californian*'s radio had been on?

After the tragedy, safety rules changed. Ships had to have enough lifeboats for all aboard. Their wireless radios

had to be on day and night. An ice patrol was formed in 1914. To this day, it warns ships about icebergs in the North Atlantic. Even today, no ship is truly unsinkable.

Chapter 3

On September 9, 1985, the *Titanic* was front-page news again. Just back from their voyage, scientists spoke to reporters.

Dr. Robert Ballard, a leader of the team that discovered the wreck

One of the team's leaders, Dr. Robert
Ballard, described the wreck. The two
biggest pieces—the bow and the stern—

were lying 1,970 feet apart. Smaller
pieces lay scattered between the two.

For now, Dr. Ballard kept one thing a secret—the exact location of the wreck. Why? He worried that others would try to find it and bring up pieces. He thought the rule should be "Look, but don't touch."

Who did the *Titanic* belong to now? No one, really. The company that built it no longer existed. Did that mean people could just take pieces of the wreck for themselves?

Dr. Ballard thought that was wrong. He would not touch the *Titanic*. In 1986, he and his team placed a plaque on the stern of the wreck in honor of those who died. It asked that the *Titanic* be left in peace.

IN MEMORY OF THOSE SOULS WHO PERISHED
WITH THE "TITANIC" APRIL 14/15, 1912.
DEDICATED TO
WILLIAM H. TANTUM, IV WHOSE DREAM TO FIND
THE "TITANIC"
HAS BEEN REALIZED
BY DR. ROBERT D. BALLARD.
THE OFFICERS AND MEMBERS OF THE
TITANIC HISTORICAL SOCIETY INC. 1986

In 1987, a US company searched the site of the wreck. Their deep-sea sub could carry three people. It had video cameras and a robotic arm. It could pick up objects from the wreck.

The deep-sea sub *Nautile* searches the wreck site.

These forks and butter knife were recovered from the wreck.

In 1987 alone, more than 1,800 objects were brought up. For better or worse, pieces of the *Titanic* were being taken from the depths.

Some *Titanic* survivors did not want pieces of the ship brought up. One of them was Eva Hart, who was seven years old in 1912. "I feel it's quite wrong," she said in 1987. "I feel it's piracy." Eva's father had died when the *Titanic* sank. She thought everything should be left just as it was. Others disagreed. They felt that pieces of history were being saved from the mud.

Chapter 4

Today, about 5,500 items have been taken from the *Titanic*. They have been cleaned and restored. The pieces are part of a traveling museum exhibit.

More than 16 million people have flocked to see the items in museums around the world. It is the closest that most people can get to actual pieces of the ship. None of them are for sale—except for small bits of coal from the wreck site.

Amazingly, many items like these dishes were not broken during the sinking. They were found lying in neat rows. However, the wooden case that held them had rotted away long before.

Most items made from paper and cloth did not last long in the water. But clothes found inside leather suitcases and bills in wallets remained protected.

Some of the papers that were found tell of passengers' plans once they arrived in the United States. As this paper shows, one person was trying to become a US citizen.

A perfume sales kit was also lifted from the ocean floor. It contained 62 glass sample bottles. Many still had perfume inside.

Some items revealed what everyday life was like on the ship. A wall telephone had instructions on it: "Press plunger to call distant station, lift right-hand tube to ear, speak close into mouthpiece."

Other items related to the story of the sinking. Part of the ship's wheel, from the bridge of the *Titanic*, was recovered. Most of the wood had rotted away over time. A crewman threw, or spun, it hard in hopes of avoiding the iceberg.

Using a telegraph like this one, an officer sent an urgent order to the engine room: "Full astern." That meant the ship had to reverse its course.

And here is the bell from the crow's nest—the very bell Frederick Fleet rang at 11:40 PM. It was the alarm that had come too late.

Chapter 5

Since 1985, scientists, filmmakers, and others have photographed, filmed, and mapped the wreck. When their images are matched up with photos of the ship from 1912, the *Titanic* comes back to life.

The boat deck was ripped in two.

A *Titanic* propeller half buried in mud

These images of the wreck become more important every day. That's because the *Titanic* is slowly breaking down. No one can say exactly how quickly it is happening. Tiny sea creatures are actually eating the iron.

If time is running out, should more of the wreck be raised? Or should everything be left in peace? The discovery of the *Titanic* answered many questions. But brand-new ones have floated up to take their place.

Time Line

April 10, 1912

12:00 PM   The *Titanic* sets sail from Southampton, England.

6:30 PM   The *Titanic* stops in Cherbourg, France. Then it sails on to Queenstown, Ireland.

April 11, 1912

1:30 PM   The ship leaves Queenstown for New York City.

April 12–13, 1912

The passengers enjoy pleasant weather.

April 14, 1912

11:40 PM   Frederick Fleet spots the iceberg. Moments later, the *Titanic* scrapes against it.

April 15, 1912

12:00 AM   Captain Smith learns the ship will sink within hours. He orders the radio operators to send out calls for help.

12:25 AM   The crew begins to help passengers into lifeboats.

12:45 AM   The first lifeboat is lowered into the water.

1:15 AM   By now, the ship is tilting with the bow very low and the stern rising.

2:05 AM   The last lifeboat is launched.

2:17 AM   The *Titanic* sends its last SOS.

2:18 AM   The ship breaks in two. The bow section sinks.

2:20 AM   The stern section fills with water, tilts again, and sinks.

4:00 AM   The *Carpathia* arrives on the scene.

8:50 AM   The *Carpathia* steams toward New York with the survivors.

April 18, 1912

9:00 PM   The *Carpathia* arrives in New York City.